THE PILLOW BOOK

EDITED AND INTRODUCED BY
CHARLES FOWKES

HAMLYN

The Hamlyn Publishing Group Limited
a division of The Octopus Publishing Group
Michelin House, 81 Fulham Road
London SW3 6RB
and distributed for them by
Octopus Distribution Services
Rushden, Northamptonshire NN10 9RZ, England

ISBN 0 600 55698 0

Printed in Hong Kong

ACKNOWLEDGEMENTS

ILLUSTRATIONS: Victor Lownes was very generous in allowing many beautiful items from his important collection of paintings and prints to be photographed and reproduced.

David May provided several fine pieces including the tantric painting, and Office du Livre in Fribourg some Chinese subjects from other private collections.

The photograph on page 51 is reproduced by kind permission of the Trustees of the Victoria and Albert Museum.

Edward Pullirsch was kind enough to allow his pillow books to be photographed: all admirers of Japanese culture are recommended to visit the shop Japanalia in Munich.

Finally, no book on Eastern erotica could be complete without some subjects from Lance Dane's unique collection.

DESIGN: Grahame Dudley designed the book and Peter MacDonald typeset it. Irene Sanderson executed the calligraphy which accompanies Ikkyu's poems.

TEXT: Indra Sinha translated the vivid extracts from Hindu love manuals from the Sanskrit; Don Sanderson made the translations of Ikkyu's poems. The folk songs from the Maikhal Hills and Chhattisgarh are part of the pioneer work done by Verrier Elwin and Shamao Hivale and are included by kind permission of Oxford University Press. Most significant of all is the debt owed to E. Powys Mathers whose translations appear in all three sections of the book. Every effort has been made to trace all copyright holders, but in some cases this has been impossible: anyone not acknowledged should write to the editor care of the publisher.

Without Victor Lownes and E. Powys Mathers this would have been much less of a book.

Contents

INTRODUCTION

China, Japan, Persia and Arabia – indeed most of the world's great cultures – have a long tradition of erotic literature. This ranges from poetry and novels to text books such as those of the Ming Dynasty in China or the more or less continuous stream of love manuals which have been produced in India since the very earliest period. Western civilization is unique in having no such tradition of erotic literature.

The absence of any continuous tradition of erotology in the West – most of the eastern cultures listed above have suffered only short periods of repression – is rather curious. Those Western writers who have gone against the tide stand out like beacons in the darkness of repression and guilt. For sex, the Dark Ages never ended (may not yet have ended).

At the highest level, as in the sparkling aphorisms of Kama Sutra, erotic instruction is as much art as poetry. Indeed it may be expressed in poetry or in the form of short stories or parables as in The Perfumed Garden. The term erotica (in literature) and erotology are, to all intents and purposes, interchangeable.

Like any other subject, sex has attracted its share of bad writers and poor artists, but the list of writers who have had anything of interest to say specifically about sex is surprisingly short. In the long centuries from the fall of Rome to the Victorian era, a list including Boccaccio, Aretino, Rabelais, Villon, Herrick, Donne, Rochester, Carew, Cleland, Casanova, is pathetically close to being complete. When the names of those whose work includes significant writing about sex is included, Chaucer, Shakespeare, La Fontaine, the list is even nearer to completion.

While Western literature made little use of sex as a subject, the thriving folk tradition was more direct and had much more in common with the folk songs of India, some of which have been included in this anthology. The following folk poems both use vegetable metaphors to deal with the male organ – impotent in the Gond song from Central India, and in a more cheerful aspect in the traditional English verse which follows:

Wild Cucumber

On the tulsi platform
The pot looks pretty
To look at you are fine as a wild cucumber
But when I eat you, how bitter you are!

Riddle of a Gooseberry

The fruit in fear some ladies pull,
'Tis smooth and round and plump and full.
It yields dear moisture, pure and thick.
It seldom makes a lady sick.

The list of pre-nineteenth century Western poets who chose sex as their subject is short enough, but instructional works of erotology do not even constitute a list. Apart from the postures described in Aretino's *Ragionamenti* (1534) and a few comments in medical books, Western civilization produced no major book on how to increase sexual pleasure or improve sexual techniques for more than a thousand years.[1]

It had not always been so. In classical times there was a huge body of Greek and Latin erotology ranging from minor instructional and analytical pieces to the works of the greatest poets and dramatists. Perhaps the most famous work of classical erotology was Ovid's Ars Amatoria (Art of Love) which is a treasure house of wit and sound advice. The erotology of Lucretius in De Rerum Natura (Of the Nature of Things) written around 54 BC is more prosaic and makes an interesting comparison to the treatment of the

same sexual posture in the Panchasayaka (Five Arrows) translated from the Sanskrit:

... Nam more ferarum
Quadrupedumque magis ritu plerumque putantur
Concipere uxores, quia sic loca summere possunt
Pectoribus positis sublatis semina lumbris.

... Women conceive more readily when down in the manner of beasts, as the organs absorb the seed best when the breast is depressed and the loins lifted.

[1] An exception to this general statement is the erotic writing of the seventeenth-century French lawyer Nicolas Chorier whose elegant Latin prose (written under the pseudonym of a Spanish lady Aloysia Siguria to excite and instruct the classically-educated gentlemen of his age) compares well with the best of the classical writers and even with the lively Sanskrit: His member swelled up, red and threatening. 'I beg of you madam, turn on your face'. I did as he said. When he saw my buttocks, whiter than ivory, he cried 'How beautiful you are! But raise yourself on your knees and bend your head down'. I bowed my head and bosom, and lifted my buttocks. He thrust his swift moving and burning dart to the bottom of my vulva and took my nipples in either hand. Then he began to work in and out and soon sent a sweet rivulet into the cavern of Venus. I felt unspeakable pleasure and nearly fainted with lust!'

अधोमुखस्थां रमयेच्च नारीं तत्पृष्ठवर्ती पशुतुल्यरूपः ।
भर्ता परिक्रीडति भावहीनो निर्दिश्यते हारिण एष बन्धः ॥

If your lustful lover buries her face in the pillow and goes on all fours like an animal and you rut upon her from behind as though you were a wild beast, this coupling is Harina, The Deer.

Erotology had its renaissance between three and four centuries late. Improved printing techniques, better communications, broader education, the growth of the middle class and other radical shifts in the power structure of society all contributed to the growth of the publishing houses and were – of course – all related. More books, meant more erotic books. Sadly, much of this output was the worst kind of crude pornography – which is still the case today.

Because writers and artists concerned with erotic subjects have often been radicals, worked on the edges of society, living in disreputable districts, there is a strong link with revolution and social change. It was in the Green Houses of the courtesans of Yoshiwara that the revolution which brought an end to 250 years of shogun domination of Japan was planned in 1867.

Two centuries earlier, the same link with radicalism found expression in the satires of John Wilmot, Earl of Rochester, for example this ribald attack on the Maid of Honour Cary Frazier, daughter of Charles II's Court physician:

Her father gave her dildos six,
Her mother made 'em up a score;
But she loves nought but living pricks,
And swears by God she'll frig no more.

The eighteenth and nineteenth century saw an enormous resurgence of erotic writing. The eighteenth century had Casanova and John Cleland and a host of others; the nineteenth century Baudelaire, and Verlaine, Rimbaud and Swinburne. The nineteenth century also had 'Walter' author of the most comprehensive and frank erotic autobiography ever written, and Richard Burton. Burton made the first serious attempt since classical times to write intelligently about erotic practices and techniques. To achieve this he used his extensive knowledge of oriental languages to translate first The Arabian Nights and subsequently Kama Sutra, Ananga Ranga and Perfumed Garden. It was the first – and still some of the best – erotology of modern times.

The twentieth century has witnessed an explosion of fiction concerned with sex and – pre and post Kinsey – a great deal of instructional erotology: much of it is uninspired and pedestrian. The Church and other pressures within Western society had created a hiatus of more than a thousand years. While occidental erotology struggles to make up lost time, the West can still look towards the East for wisdom and inspiration – as it has always done.

客散曲終無一声
不知極睡幾時驚
覿面当機胡蝶戯
誰聞日午打三更

The guests have left, the music ended, there is no sound;
One cannot tell when she will awake from this profound sleep;
Now as I watch, a butterfly plays.
Listen, the bell strikes midnight at noon.

The illustrations in this book are from as wide a variety of sources as the text. Some come from the bazaars of eastern cities, others from the courts of princes. They represent every shade of feeling from tenderness to lust, and every shade of expression from the naive to the sophisticated and arch. Some images are fine works of art, others are cheerfully rude. All record an aspect of sex, many of love.

Tantric artists in India were tapping the deep well of the subconscious long before Salvador Dali and the Surrealists in the West. It is sometimes suggested that Tantrism – with its orgiastic rituals – bears the same relation to Hinduism and Buddhism as black magic to Christianity. But the imitative nastiness of black magic cannot bear comparison with the intellectual and artistic legacy of Tantrism.

INDIA

How should we quench love when there is fire
even in the pollen of the lotus under water,
even in wet sandal essence, even in the
dew of the frozen lantern of the moon?

AMARU

THE CROW

If, lying side by side, you simultaneously kiss each other's secret parts it is the lovemaking of the Crow, a sexual technique much practised by slaves, itinerants and other low persons.

विपर्ययेन शयितौ नायकौ तु परस्परम् ॥
चुम्बतो युगपत् स्थानं तत्काकिलरतं भवेत् ।
रतिकाले प्रयोज्यत्वाद्रत्यङ्गत्वात्तथापि च ॥

RATIRATNAPRADIPIKA

The Ratiratnapradipika love manual dates from the fifteenth century and is thought to have been written by the Maharaja Prandha Devaraya.

Amaru is the supreme love poet of Sanskrit literature. His dates are unknown but he was certainly writing before 800 AD. Mayura, whose poetry at its best rivals Amaru, is an even more shadowy figure but of approximately the same period.

SANGARA

Her mouth quickens now upon the shaft; when you stir to her lips and tongue-tip, she swallows it as deeply as she can and kisses when you cry out: this is Sangara, Swallowed Up.

जिह्वाग्रेणावपीड्यौष्ठव्यापारेण च सत्वरम् ।
यावच्छुक्रागमं चैव वषट्कृत्यावचुम्बयेत् ॥
तदेतत्सङ्गरं ख्यातमौपरिष्टकमुच्यते ।
कुलटा स्वैरिणी वेश्या दासी च परिचारिका ॥

RATIRATNAPRADIPIKA

BAHUCHUSHITA

Seat your lover upon a dais, lift her feet to your shoulders, clasp her buttocks, let your tongue moisten love's temple and stir it to overflowing: this is Bahuchushita, Sucked Hard.

मञ्चोपरिस्थकान्तायाः पदयुग्ममधस्स्थितः ।
नायकः स्कन्धयोर्धृत्वा कराभ्यां तत्कटिस्थलम् ॥
आलिङ्ग्य च स्वरसनाक्षोभितस्मरमन्दिरम् ।
तत्सम्भूतं रतिजलं बहुशोऽप्यवचूषयेत् ॥
तदौपरिष्टकं ज्ञेयं बहुचूषितँसंज्ञकम् ।

RATIRATNAPRADIPIKA

Oral lovemaking techniques were not dealt with in detail until the Middle Ages. The Ratiratnapradipika was obviously influenced by Tantrism (see Introduction) and gives the fullest account of fellatio and cunnilingus in Hindu erotic writing. The ancient texts placed less emphasis on the Auparishtaka, or mouth congress, although the practice is a perennial favourite. With typical pragmatism, Vatsyayana in Kama Sutra describes orality as the prerogative of eunuchs and 'wanton women', but adds that in love everybody should act 'according to his own inclination'.

With anxious eyes she looks with longing at him, and forgets the blow
He too forgets at once and stretches out his hand to pick the lemons of her tree.
He eats them both and his mouth is full of nectar.
He passes through the mango grove to the little secret well:
Parting the grasses by the mouth he lets down his silver bucket...
'Oh master, I am tired. You have pounded me till I am as soft as a seedless mango.
There is no juice left in me. Now let me sleep a little'.

'Who has used my well, Rani? The brim of my well is wet, Rani'.

'I was dying of thirst, Raja; and thus the brim of your well is wet, Raja'.

'Who has eaten my mangoes, Rani? The rinds are fresh, Rani'.

'The gardener's wife, brought them Raja, And so the rinds are fresh, Raja'.

In quite a different oral tradition are the wonderful folk songs of India. Not only do these poems offer an interesting contrast to the high art of Amaru, or the extracts from ancient and medieval Hindu love manuals, they are remarkable both for their frank treatment of sexuality and the erotic symbolism which colours many (among some of the peoples of Middle India it would be reasonable to say most) of the songs. The first poem on this page is from The Story of Dhola, in the second Raja Rasalu suspects Rani Kokilan of being unfaithful in a legend from the Punjab.

THE KNEE ELBOW

If you lift the girl by passing your elbows under her knees and enjoy her as she hangs trembling with her arms garlanding your neck, it is called Janukurpura, the Knee-Elbow.

कूर्परद्वितयकेन योषितो जानुकण्ठमवलम्ब्य संस्थितः ।
तस्य मध्यमवलम्ब्य सा रमेज्जानुकूर्परमुदाहरन्ति तत् ॥

RATIRATNAPRADIPIKA

The koel longs for a mango
And my life longs for you
I cannot hold my life in patience
Your body is like a plantain stalk
Sweet as a divided mango

TRADITIONAL SONG

The 'koel' in the fragment of folk song from the Maikal Hills is the Indian cuckoo which is often used in village poetry as the symbol for a lover. The imagery of the last poem is strongly reminiscent of that used by the Hebrew poet in the Song of Songs:

'As the apple tree among the trees of the wood,
So is my beloved among the sons.
I sat down under his shadow with great delight,
And his fruit was sweet to my taste'.

The legs are of saja

The frame is of sarai

O girl with tinkling bells

I will make music

On your bed tonight!

Folk song from Belha,
Bilaspur Tahsil

Churning Curds

Caging your lover in your arms, you part her knees and sink into her, crushing her body to yours: this is known as Dadhyataka, or Churning Curds.

अन्योन्यदोःपञ्जरमध्ययाताः स्तम्भं यदा जानुयुगेन मग्नाः ।
निष्पीड्य नारी पतिमध्यसंस्था रमेत दध्यायतकं वदन्ति(६) ॥

Panchasayaka

Instead of the deep blue lotus her glance to him, her teeth in a lighted smile instead of the jasmine, instead of the cup one moving breast of hers. Thus, though she has little means, she finds a celebration for his return.

Amaru

The Hindu couple below are equal: they take pleasure in each other, give pleasure to each other. The painting of their lovemaking records, instructs and gives pleasure to us – across the centuries and across cultures. It is erotic, it gives something back to life: it is the antithesis of pornography which only takes away from life and is no more than a bleak dead end.

Suavely the wine pouring from your lower lip has called the golden swarm. It is a crimson fruit and has called the bees. The boy who has sucked that carmine fruit is drunken, and I am drunken, and the gilded bees.

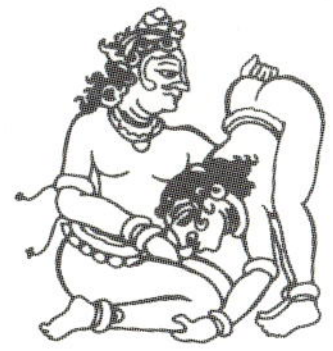

MAYURA

THE BLACK BEE

If you lie flat with your lover astride you, her feet drawn up and her hips revolving so that your penis circles deep within her sex, it is Bhramara, the Black Bee.

ANANGA RANGA

Bees and honey have been a rich source of imagery for writers from all cultures; from the very earliest times the unsuspecting insect has provided endless symbolic possibilities from the sacred to the profane, and few creatures can rival its position in mythology and literature. The lovemaking position depicted in the painting and described above is known as 'the bee'. Mayura's magnificent poem explores the erotic possibilities, while the wedding chant from Phuljhar humorously describes one bee's revenge for being made the vehicle for so much human cerebration.

Cut off the top
Of the honeycomb
A bee has stung
The bride's vagina

VILLAGE SONG

When she lifts her thighs and you sit astraddle them, your knees tightly clamped, kissing her tenderly and riding saddle upon her buttocks, this is Shankha, the Conch.

कान्तानितंबभागात्पुरतो विधृतार्धदेहभागः सन् ।
दृढबन्धनिश्चलाङ्गश्चुंबन् रतिमेति शङ्खबन्धं तत् ॥

SRINGARARASAPRABANDHADIPIKA

Last night my kisses drowned in the softness of black hair
And my kisses like bees went plundering the softness of black hair.
Last night my hands were thrust in the mystery of black hair,
And my kisses like bees went plundering the sweetness of pomegranates.
And among the scents of the harvest above my queen's neck the harvest of black hair.
And my teeth played with the golden skin of her two ears.
Last night my kisses drowned in the softness of black hair
And my kisses like bees went plundering the softness of black hair.

AFGHAN POEM

Hair offers even more direct possibilities for erotic symbolism than the bees of the preceding pages although the industrious insects reappear in the Afghan poem above.

The great lady from Kotah depicted in the painting has loosened her hair in passion, not as the poor Dom girl in the Shyam Ray ballad: Welcoming her princely lover to her humble hut, she has only one way of making her rough couch soft, 'should you feel pain I will spread my long and flowing hair in the bed to make it easy for you'. The European imagination has explored the complex symbolism of hair in texts as diverse as Rapunzel and Alexander Pope's Rape of the Lock (and of course – when the fetish becomes an end in itself – in the work of Krafft-Ebing and Freud).

Rain scents of the coupling of trees come to the assembly of poets again. You went to bathe in the river, and I took new interest in the King's stallion. He roared for the quick mares to be brought to him, he drummed with his forelegs upon them. O woman moist with a boy's love!

Mayura

The Mare's Trick

When, straightening her legs, she grips and milks your penis with her vagina, as a mare holds a stallion, it is Vadavaka, the Mare, which is not learned without practice.

सम्पुटके योषिच्चेद्योन्योष्ठाभ्यां गृहीतयुवदण्डा ।
उद्धृत्यैतस्य पुनर्मुञ्चेत्सङ्गृह्य वाडवं करणम् ॥

Ratiratnapradipika

The horse has a very special place in Indian mythology: not only were the original Aryan invaders a 'horse culture', so too were the later Muslim conquerors. In the Ramayana, Kausalya touches a stallion to ensure the birth of a son. In all horse cultures the animal becomes a powerful symbol; its appearance and behaviour the object of study. The amusing precision (and variety) with which the Norman ladies depicted the penises of their husbands' war horses in the Bayeux tapestry gives a clue to the peculiarly intimate relationship which develops between humans and horses in warrior societies. The sister of Sir Philip Sidney (the perfect courtier) is known to have enjoyed watching horses mate, as are Pope Alexander VI and his daughter Lucretzia who watched the performance regularly at the Vatican 'cum magno risu et delectatione'. Mayura's poem suggests that the practice is not rare: Sheikh Nefzawi even recommends it as a potent aphrodisiac in his Perfumed Garden.

Riding is, of course, the most commonplace of sexual metaphors. The Gond and Pardhan tribes of India say 'When we see a horse, we think of sex'. From the earliest time, the sexual technique depicted on the opposite page has been known as 'the Mare's trick'.

The Pestle

Stretched out like a pole in the middle of the bed, she lies joined to you in lovemaking, her breathless cries mounting as you polish the jewel of her clitoris: this is Mausala, the Pestle.

दण्डवद्युगलं शय्या मध्यमे रतिमेष्यति ।
कूजितैर्मणितैर्हीनं मौसलं बन्धमुच्यते ॥

Sringararasaprabandhadipika

By the sixty paps of Bhavita, I tell you he deceived you with Narayani, and I surprised them. Yesterday he took hold of my breasts by guile. Do you hear that? He took hold of my breasts. Also he kissed me by force this morning and tore my lips.

You lie!

Look at these wounds.

I cannot believe my eyes. I must taste them. I must taste them.

Amaru

How can I go into the inner room?

My anklets sound chunur chunur.

The wheat bread is soft

The oil drips from it!

O lover, eat, and you will be content

My anklets sound chunur chunur.

FOLK SONG, MAIKAL HILLS

Since your husband has got to depart at dawn, listen to me carefully. He must not see your joy; you must weep, and keep him; you must tell him that you have not the courage to stay in a room his absence leaves most desolate; you must go out and see to his horse, and bid the servant saddle the fastest.

AMARU

The Cobra

If, lying with her face turned away, the fawn-eyed girl offers you her buttocks and your penis enters the house of love, this is Nagabandha, the coupling of the Cobra.

पार्श्वे स्थिताया मृगशावकाक्ष्याः पृष्ठावलम्बी(१०) रमणः प्रसुप्तः।
लिङ्गस्मरागारनिवेशयोगादिहोपदिष्टः किल नागबन्धः ॥
इति पार्श्वबन्धसमुद्देशः ॥

Panchasayaka

Lovely Lady

She whose dark eyes are like fallen lotus petals takes your penis and guides it into her vulva, then clings tight to you and shakes her buttocks, this is Charunarikshita, Lovely Lady In Charge.

उत्तानास्यांभोजपत्रायताक्षी भर्तुर्लिङ्गं पाणिनाधाय योनौ ।
श्लिष्यन्ती चेच्चालयेत्स्वं नितंबं बन्धः प्रोक्तश्चारुनारीक्षितो ऽयं ॥१७५

Ratikallolini

'Pity!' she says, with bruised breasts and disordered hair. With eyes closed and legs still trembling, 'Finish!' she says. She says in a choked voice: 'It is enough!' And now her silence grows eternal. Is she dead or sleeping, is she meditating in delight on what has happened, or thinking of another?

Amaru

China

Purple Fire Lady heated some wine, passing it from her mouth to his, tickling his tongue with hers. Hsi-Men Ch'ing, thirsty for another wine, knelt and pressed his tongue deep into the purple cup set in alabaster. A magic cup! The more he drank, the more it filled.

The tongue he found lacked eloquence in words, but not in sighs.

The maid had left a lamp on the table. In the game called Claws of the Dragon, Hsi-Men could look down and see red enter white, hard enter soft. Again and again, in the game whose end is dreaded and yet longed for, the pattern was repeated: until Purple Fire Lady, noisy from both mouths, became quiet and turned her autumn-glancing eyes to him.

金瓶梅

The Chin P'ing Mei (Golden Lotus) was placed on the list of prohibited books from the moment of its first publication at the end of the seventeenth century – although the brother of the Emperor K'ang Hsi thought the novel sufficiently interesting to translate it into Manchu. It was written more than a hundred years earlier by Wang Shih-cheng, although other hands added to it in manuscript. The Chin P'ing Mei is therefore a work from the end of the Ming Dynasty, but deals with the life of an upper class family of the twelfth century (the Sung). No doubt this was to protect the author from prosecution as – in addition to its frank sexual descriptions – it is a ruthless expose of bureaucratic corruption. Wang Shih-cheng was himself involved in politics, and there is a tradition that he poisoned the pages of the manuscript and gave it to Yen Shih-fan, the Prime Minister. The intention was that his enemy would become engrossed in reading the book and absorb the poison as he turned the pages.

Whatever the original intentions of the author the Chin P'ing Mei is a fine novel. Cordier's Bibliotheca Sinica says that it describes 'a whole company of men and women in all the different relationships that arise in social life and we see them pass successively through all the situations through which civilized human beings can pass...such a book would render superfluous any other book upon the manners of the Chinese'.

The Chinese have never regarded novel writing as a proper occupation for men of literature. Consequently none of the time-honoured literary conventions applied to novels, which were written in abbreviated colloquial language. This plain, unembellished style means that individuals are not described by the author: they come alive through their words and actions. In this respect there are similarities to Greek tragedy, except that the Chin P'ing Mei does not deal with the important issues of human existence but with day-to-day life in a wealthy, polygamous household during the reign of Hui Tsung (AD 1101-1126). The Golden Lotus is nearer to soap opera than Greek tragedy, with the important difference that it is scrupulously, and often bleakly, truthful.

The passages which follow are those concerned with the sexual behaviour of Hsi-Men Ch'ing, the central character of the novel. Of course there is much more to the Chin P'ing Mei than that; but the author pursued Hsi-Men Ch'ing into the bedroom and it suits the purposes of this book to follow him there....

Late into the summer night, Hsi-men Ch'ing and his ladies enjoyed themselves in the scented seclusion of the flower arbour. When at last it was time to go to bed, the master of the house was flushed with wine and aching to enjoy Golden Lotus. His principal wife, Moon Lady, went discreetly to her room while the master and the new arrival eagerly undressed. Incense was burned and the bed curtains pulled back.

Golden Lotus played the flute exquisitely, but that was not the instrument she placed between her lips. For a long time she played softly, the pleasure of Hsi-men Ch'ing becoming unendurable. At last, deft fingering tormented a cascade of music from the pipe, while Hsi-men Ch'ing dissolved in bliss.

金瓶梅

Chin P'ing Mei

Moonbeam passed fruit, sweet with honey, from her mouth to his. She took another fruit with dainty fingers and began caressing it with her tongue.

Taking it out of her mouth from time to time she marvelled at its deep purple colour and firmness, before slipping it back between her lips. Its juice too was sweet to her taste. Then it was time to pass that fruit to another mouth.

Hsi-men had more wine while she washed. It was still snowing outside.

In bed he was hot against her cold washed body, firm against her softness. Soon both were warm. It was the first night watch before they were finished.

金瓶梅

CHIN P'ING MEI

Now his mind was heated with wine and the chase, and another game occurred to him. It was more wicked than before and suited to the name of his accomplice.

Hsi-men told the maid Plum Blossom to watch: 'we shall call the game Hitting a Silver Swan with a Golden Ball'. He took a small plum and asked Golden Lotus to open her mouth. 'No, not that mouth!' She understood and laughed, and with her fingers opened the petals of the flower.

Three times he tried, throwing gently and failing. Only when Golden Lotus became excited by the sport – and even a little snail came out to see the game – did a plum catch in the moist folds. No sooner there than removed and replaced with another plum: larger, more intense in colour – and still on the stalk.

Golden Lotus closed her eyes in delight.

金瓶梅 *Chin P'ing Mei*

When Hsi-men returned from washing, Golden Lotus was naked on the cushions. In the heat she fanned her white limbs with a white fan, but her shoes were crimson.

Naked himself, Hsi-men wriggled his toes in another crimson shoe. Then, setting to work more seriously, he made his little plaything glisten under his fingers, the crimson opening slippery with nectar on his tongue.

The need too urgent, they played the oldest, fiercest game: The Arrow through the Arch. Soon they were lost in the sounds and smells and tastes of battle. At the moment of his victory, which was hers also, Golden Lotus cried out from under him: 'Darling, Darling!' It was her battle cry.

Chin P'ing Mei

金瓶梅

Golden Lotus took the sweet-smelling flower and put it in her hair. Content, she walked towards the inner courtyard, leaving Hsi-men Ch'ing alone with Vase Lady.

The summer sunlight made a mockery of her silk skirt, and of the silk trousers she wore beneath, revealing her white flesh to Hsi-men. His passion roused, he lifted her skirt, pulled down her silken trousers, bringing hardness and softness together.

Crossing the Mountains with Fire was the game they played...

They did not hear Golden Lotus return, but she heard them. She heard his words as he praised her soft white behind, and she heard his belly slapping it, and she heard the cries they made at the last.

Chin P'ing Mei

金瓶梅

When you sat in your dark chair
Ripe with fat fruits of yellow and red silk
Alive with blue lithe animals.

Pressing your scented rose-ended
Peach-coloured feet against my face,
I was humiliated, as you desired.

Nineteenth-century poem

Feet and shoes have kept the psychologists, folklorists and anthropologists almost as busy as hair. The notorious practice of compressing the feet of women to keep them small was widespread in China until the twentieth century and – not surprisingly – feet play an important part in Chinese erotic art and literature. It does not seem to have been a national epidemic of foot fetishism so much as an alternative object of secondary sexual interest: small feet in China being analagous to ample breasts in the West. Although, if the nineteenth-century anthropologist Matignan is to be believed, there may have been rather more to it than that: 'All the Celestials (Chinese) whom I have interrogated on this point have replied unanimously: 'Oh, a little foot! You Europeans cannot understand how exquisite, how sweet, how exciting it is!' The contact of the genital organ with the little foot produces in the male an indescribable degree of voluptuous feeling, and women skilled in love know that to arouse their lovers a better method than all Chinese aphrodisiacs.... is to take the penis between the feet. It is not rare to find Chinese Christians accusing themselves at Confession of having had evil thoughts on looking at a woman's foot'. A tiny foot may have been a 'golden water lily' for Chinese men, but the misery suffered by generations of women is incalculable.

JAPAN

我手何似森手
自信公風流主
発病治玉茎萌
且喜我会裏衆

My hand, would that it resembled Mori's hand

My faithful lady's, the mistress of love's caress

When I am ill she heals my precious stalk

And brings joy to my circle of followers.

Ikkyu

Nightingale to Plum Tree

How the Nightingales sing to the
plum trees
And the frogs splash in the water.
That is love.
The call of people and of things
Is everywhere.

Dark Clouds,
Fishing boats,
At the will of the tide,
At the will of the wind.

Geisha song

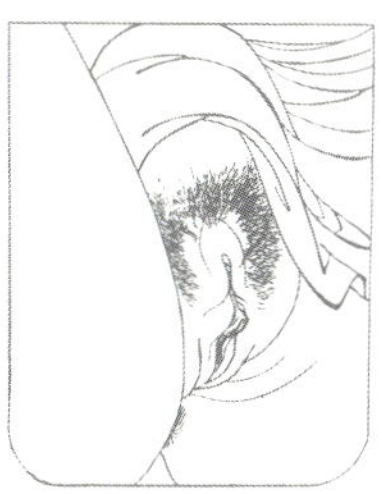

SOUTH-EAST QUARTER

Light affairs become frivolous
At Fukagawa,
My body is frivolous.

A thin uncoloured chord on the samisen.

In intimate Nakatcho Street
Affairs are private,
And the news of our love
Spreads gallantly,
The way of the South-East.

Two lovers are in the little room
And the screen has double hinges.

We pretend worldly fidelity,
Painting moles on each other.

Perhaps
We shall know in heaven.

GEISHA SONG

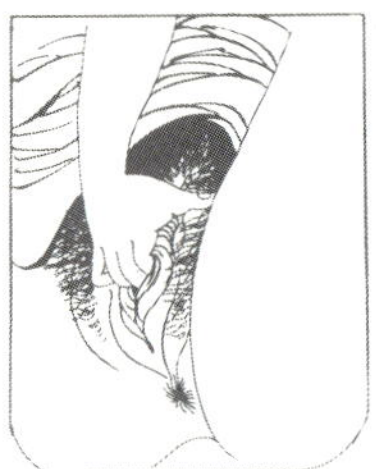

Ikkyu was a Zen monk, reputed to have been the illegitimate son of the Emperor Gokomatsu. Active during the greater part of the fifteenth century (he died aged eighty-seven) his Kyounshu – a collection of more than a thousand poems written in Chinese – is one of the great treasures of Japanese literature. The poems are of three types: those concerned with the doctrines of Zen Buddhism; those criticising contemporary abuses – and the love poems. Some biographers, embarrassed at a monk who wrote of 'licking his lover's sexual sweetness' have sought to 'explain' these fiercely erotic poems as forming part of the second category. Others have suggested that 'Zen' and 'love' were one and the same thing in Ikkyu's mind: in a Freudian sense they were of course, but that is not to say that they were religious poems. This is the same pious wrong-headedness which maintains that the Song of Songs in the Bible is a parable for Christ's love of the Church. Ikkyu's psychology seems to have been closer to that of John Donne – a powerful intellect which embraced love in all its forms and expressed the joys and conflicts in poetry.

臨済児孫不識禅
正伝真个瞎驢辺
雲雨三生六十劫
秋風一夜百千年

Rinzai's disciples don't understand Zen,
The truth was passed down to this blind donkey.
Making love for three lifetimes, ten eons;
One night's autumn breeze a thousand centuries.

IKKYU

Blackness

The night is black
And I am excited about you.
My love climbs in me, and you ask
That I should climb to the higher room.
Things are hidden in a black night.
Even the dream is black
On the black-lacquered pillow
Even our talk is hidden.

Geisha song

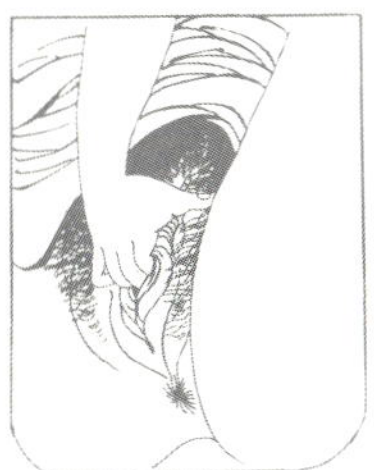

The reference to the 'black-lacquered pillow' is a reminder that the Japanese pillow was quite unlike its Western counterpart: pillow books were sometimes kept inside pillows.

楚台応望更応攀
半夜玉床愁夢間
花綻一茎梅樹下
淩波仙子遶腰間

Gaze at Chu's pavilion and then climb up to it.
At midnight on the precious bed, between dreams of sad longing
Her flower opens beneath the plum tree's branch
A graceful nymph between her thighs.

IKKYU

茆廬話到壽陽宮
胡蝶優遊興不空
枕上梅花窓外月
吟魂夜々約春風

Talk in the reed hut reaches the Shou-yang Palace.

Butterflies elegantly sport, their excitement never spent.

On the bed, a plum blossom; outside the window, the moon.

Singing souls, night after night, entwined in the spring breeze.

IKKYU

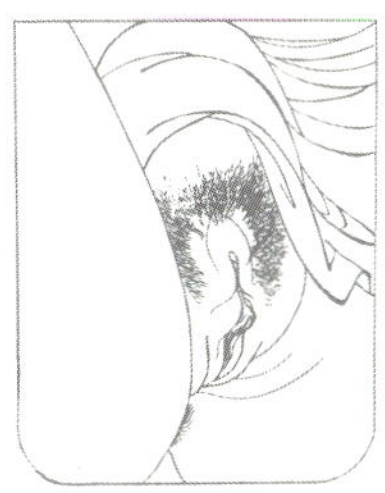

Bed

Under the unnecessarily large

Mosquito curtain

My little heart

Is fiercer than a nightlight.

Geisha song

Return

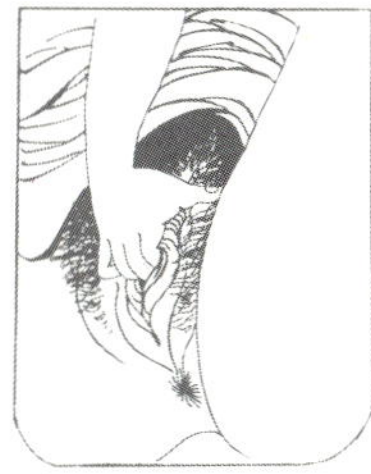

I know she is light and faithless,

But she has come back half repentant

And very pale and very sad.

A butterfly needs somewhere to rest

At evening.

Geisha song

夢迷上苑美人森
枕上梅花々信心
満口清香清浅水
黄昏月色柰新吟

Dream-wandering in the garden of beautiful Mori,
A plum blossom in the bed, faith at the heart of the flower.
My mouth is filled with the pure fragrance of that shallow stream
Dusk and the shades of the moon as we make our new song.

Ikkyu

After the death of his mentor Keso Sodon in 1428 Ikkyu began a series of wanderings. War and civil strife continually displaced Ikkyu until, in old age, he met the great love of his life, the blind servant Mori. Most of his best love poems are addressed to her.

Deep Light

I have no wish for
A frivolous or coquettish existence,
I want the deep life of love.

I have set up the double screen
Against a wind balmed with the
plum trees.

Come to me and I will love you
In the tender light of a veiled moon,
I will love you, far from the plum
trees.

Yet afterwards in bed
I know I shall sulk and weep;
Frogs in the garden pool
All night, all night.

Geisha song

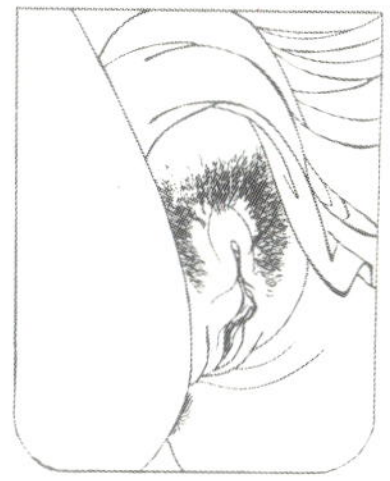

'Geisha' is a Sino-Japanese word meaning 'a person of pleasing accomplishments'. Today, geishas still belong to the strictly controlled guild which existed as early as AD 1000 and perhaps earlier. Geishas were not prostitutes: all received intensive training in dancing, singing and other traditional arts. Geishas could expect to marry well or to become the concubine of a wealthy man. Often they were more cultured and intelligent than their male clients which must have caused a degree of frustration. The essential ambiguity of their position, the endless hours of waiting which characterized their profession, and the literary skills which were part of their training caused a great deal of poetry to be written. Many of these poems were tinged with eroticism, while others explored the problems of love in a highly structured, male-dominated society.

Prediction

A hole in the paper wall
Who has been so guilty?
Through it I hear the breaking of a samisen string,
Meaning bad luck.

Yet the prediction-seller says
That mine is excellent.

Hiding Place

No more grieving.
I hide myself in my happiness
As a firefly
Hides in a moon ray.

The samisen is a traditional stringed instrument similar to a lute: it is played with an axe-shaped plectrum and has tunings designed to allow for the maximum use of open strings. All the geisha songs in this anthology were written in a free form to be accompanied by the samisen. The samisen is also part of the traditional musical accompaniment to Noh theatre.

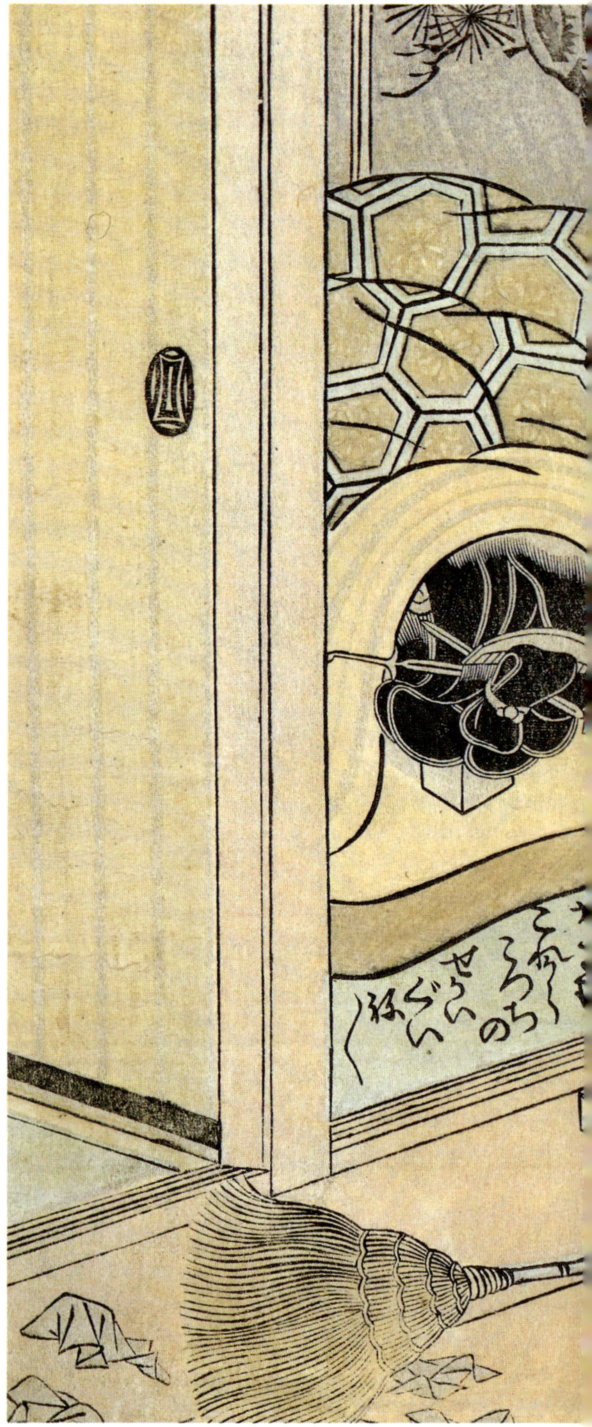

洞房深處幾詩情
歌吹花前芳宴清
雲雨枕頭江海意
鴛鴦水宿送殘生

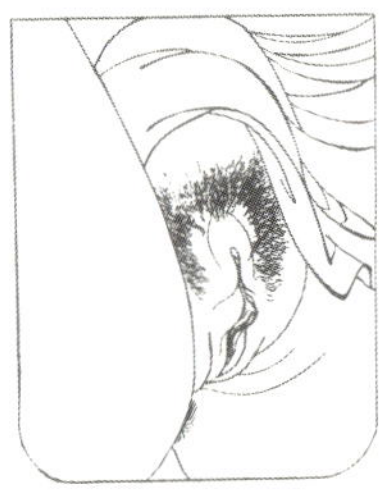

Deep in the boudoir, how much poetic feeling.

A song before the wind-blown flowers, the purity of this fragrant banquet.

Making love on the bed, a feeling of the river and the sea.

To spend the rest of our lives like mandarin ducks, at ease on the water.

Ikkyu

There is a legend that at the age of twenty-six Ikkyu achieved enlightenment on hearing a crow cry at midnight. Despite a life-long addiction to the other activities of the night, his life and work were characterised by an unshakeable belief in Zen.

Surungi Lake

Dew from the lotuses

Of Surungi Lake

Goes up in a light fume.

My hope becomes lighter than air

And disappears.

Yet a voice is saying: 'Who knows?'

Soon he may marry you.

Geisha song

The paintings in the Japanese section of this book originate from the pleasure districts of Japan's great cities: Kyoto had Shimbara, Osaka had Shimmachi and Edo, which was to become Tokyo, had the most famous and notorious of them all – 'the floating world' of Yoshiwara. Although these pleasure districts were devoted above all to the pleasures of sex they were far-removed from the shabby red-light districts of modern cities. Sexual pleasure for all tastes and pockets was available in abundance: lotus girls who pleased tradesmen manually and cheaply; young men for the samurai and great courtesans who lived in the Green Houses. But the 'city without night' was also a cultural centre where aesthetic as well as physical needs could be satisfied. Many of Japan's greatest artists lived and worked in the pleasure district, as did the publishers and printers – a fact which accounts for the quality and richness of Japan's erotic art.

Maple Leaves

Do you know why the Autumn moon

Spreads her desirable brightness

On the hill?

It is so that we two may count the leaves

of the maple

Falling

One by one.

密啓自慙私語盟
風流吟罷約三生
生身墮在畜生道
絶勝潙山戴角情

Whispers, bashfulness and a pledge
We sing of love and make promises for
three lives to come
We may fall to the way of beasts while
still alive
But I shall surpass in passion the horned
abbot of Kuei.

羽衣

Bindweed

Every morning
You flower with new colours
And garland the well bucket,
Your petals are eyes
Blinded with dew.

You are delightful

Flower long, flower differently,
Emerald cup.

Faith

I am the ordinary cherry tree
Whose flower is single.
It blossoms in the plain.

I am not one of those double
cherry trees!

Geisha songs

A woman is like a samisen –

Practise to make her strings vibrate

Better a lonely hangata

Than the penis of an oaf!

TRADITIONAL SAYINGS

A solicitous lover searches for the elusive clitoris of his mistress. Visual humour sometimes lightens the erotic work of Japan's artists but the captions are generally written in a tedious and impoverished style. They were usually added later, and seldom match the quality of the prints. The 'hangata' of the second saying above is an artificial phallus or dildo.

Blind Mori night after night sings with me
Under the covers, like mandarin ducks, new
intimate talk
Making promises to be together till the
dawning of Maitreya's salvation
At the home of this old buddha all is spring.

IKKYU

盲森夜々伴吟身
被底鴛鴦私語新
新約慈尊三会暁
本居古仏万般春

Maitreya is the future Buddha. At present he is a Bodhisattva: a compassionate inspirer and consoler of mankind who dwells in heaven and leads souls to paradise. It is prophesied that he will be born in the distant future when human virtue has become great: Ikkyu's metaphor is plain enough.

In one of Ikkyu's most famous poems he makes the charming suggestion that an excited woman has the perfume of jonquil. The plum is a rather good emblem of the male organ and appears in Japanese erotic poetry in different guises as plum branch, or plum blossom according to the demands of the moment. The caption to the nicely observed print is banal although it tells us that the man is gazing at the moon.

水仙華

香与梅花修約盟
風流瑤草両三茎
淩波仙子秦雲雨
碧海青天夜々情

Jonquil

Her perfume mixes with my plum blossom;
we pledge ourselves
A caress like two or three stalks of Yao grass
She makes love like a graceful river nymph
This feeling night after night, the sapphire
sea, azure sky.

Ikkyu

Getting out of Bed

He rises and goes. There are
Rather dark clouds.
Shall I be noisy cricket
Or firefly burning in silence.
Dumb grief or tearful parting?

And when I think we might
Never have met,
Been utter strangers…

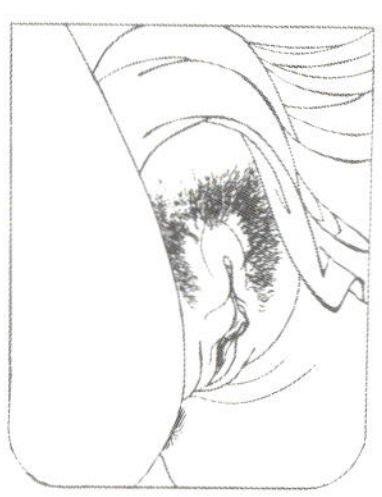

Joy

Visitor this evening
We run up the long corridor
Clicking of clogs.

Only one man,
Only one person to be loved.

I go back to my room,
Retreat, honour,
Lacquered pillow,
Silence.

I hear the watchman's rattle,
Laughter in the next room.

Geisha songs

Kawai, Kawai

(My dear, my dear)

The firefly singing not
Burns in silence;
She suffers more
Than the loud insect who says:
'Kawai, kawai!'
Why have I given all my soul
To a man without sincerity?
I regret it. I rather regret it.

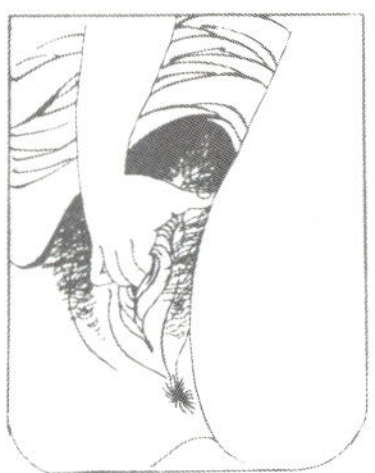

Before my Birds

I moan for love
Before my birds.
They also are in a cage.

My small complaints
Are sorry like mouse cries.
The birds hop forward to tease me
And I like it
Being so shut in.

The sake is cold
Because my torment
Makes me inefficient.
There is such a thing as great grief,
Such a thing as
Being shut in.

The lady in the print is a courtesan and before the tide of passion swept over them had been complaining about her protector's lack of fidelity.

Two Fan Game

Two thrown fans
Have fallen across each other
It is a good sign.

I see two mortals close in each
other's arms
Like two leaves fallen together.

Will he be a fine chrysanthemum?
I will put him in a vase
And look at him
He will be plum blossom
Having both scent and colour.

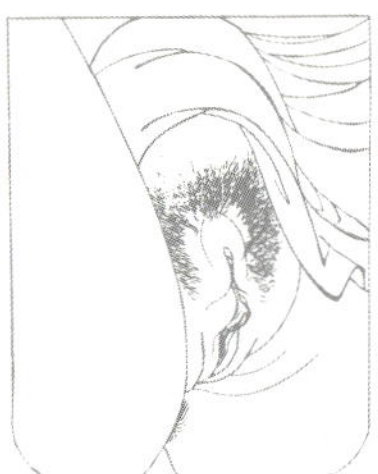

His Pretty Gesture

Because of his pretty gesture
I have fallen completely in love with him.

My letter written in common character
Will be worth more than a verbal message.
But I may not hold him yet.
I am going to drink sake all night
Without bothering to warm it.

I lie down on the floor
Just where I am, and sleep.
I wake with a start
To hear the night watch crying:
'Fire, take care of fire'.

Geisha songs

Spring Night

This dream of a Spring Night
Grows complicated
The smell of his body lies on the
air.
The cloudy sky and my ringed eyes
Are veiled.
Are we not a couple
Made of flower and butterfly?

The lady in the print wants him one more time. Her lover is taking a potent aphrodisiac with immediate and spectacular results.

The male preoccupation with penile size – and the corresponding female interest in the dramatic possibilities of prodigious sexual equipment – are reflected in all Eastern erotic art. But in Japan the artist's brush becomes – or delineates – a magic wand. It is not simply that the Japanese tradition is more erotic, the images more extreme: the penis is an object of worship in Shintoism. Even today, the male emblem, in all its variety of forms, can be seen everywhere in the countryside; in the primal creation myth a giant penis ejaculated the islands of Japan.

Myosotis

If I clasp my hands, my sleeve:
Dew and perfume and colour.
His picture remains in absence
Myosotis, memory.
If he flowered on a branch
I would plant him,
And love him every
Lonely hour.

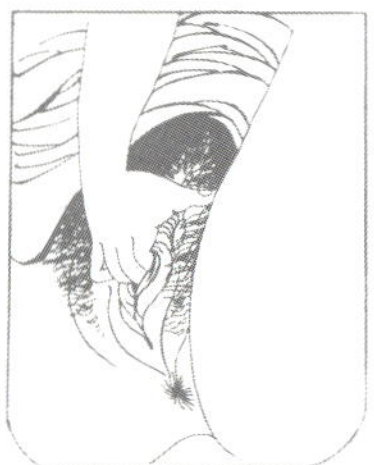

有時江海有時山
世外道人名利間
夜々鴛鴦禅榻被
風流私語一身閑

Sometimes rivers and oceans, sometimes mountains
I am an unworldly hermit, apart from fame and profit
Night after night, like mandarin ducks, under the covers on a Zen bed
That feeling, talking intimately, totally relaxed.

IKKYU

Cats

With no care for duty or people
Or strange looks at the opinion
of other cats,
One striped and the other white
Go on the edge of the roof
Or climb to the ridge of it.

Driven by the need of love
Which is stronger than death.

One day the wind of Autumn shall come
And they will not know each other.
My soul, I envy the love of cats.

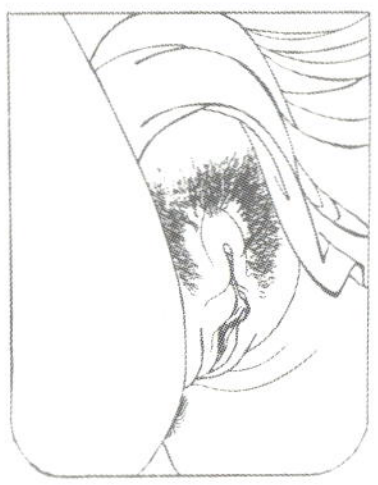

Unstable Love

Love is unstable. I dream of a drifting
Barque. My body is limited.
My thought is infinite.
Things do not go as I would have them.
I see him in the dream of a light sleep
Or resting on one arm in place of a pillow.

Audible are the bells of Mii.

The device of the two copper plums

With silver in them

Slowly and very slowly

Satisfies.

Just as all finishes

Dew falls on my clenched hand.

I would rather the bean flowered yellow

And he were here!